Strength Is Forever

AF226239

Strength Is Forever:
A Book of Poems

Nadine Dunseith

Copyright 2020 by Nadine Dunseith

All rights reserved. Published in Canada.

Trade Paperback ISBN: 978-1-7773829-1-9
eBook available in select digital stores

To Celine

May her light continue to shine

Contents

Prologue

Part 1: Courage

Part 2: Reality

Part 3: Strength

Prologue

Writing poetry has been a journey for me. I started writing not long after my friend of 22 years passed away from breast cancer. For several months, I was not sure what to write or whether I would have the words to express pain and grief. Sometimes, the right words do not come until you are ready to face them. I discovered that my only vehicle of expression was poetry.

For this compilation of poetry, I approached it from three phases in my journey as a poet. The first is the courage to write my own story of pain and grief – and the courage to face the expression of my feelings. The second phase is the reality of the pain I have faced and the memories of my life, ones I cannot deny and ones that I embrace as part of my story. The last part of my journey is the strength to carry on. Despite the experiences I've had in my childhood around sexual abuse, the path I've taken in my 20's to start over in another province, and my current reality of facing loss and anxiety, I have learned to accept these moments as part of my journey to self-awareness.

In reflecting on my journey, I have come to appreciate all the obstacles and challenges in my life – and not fear the emotions associated with them.

I have the strength to move forward. I only hope the words I write can help others as well.

Strength is forever.

PART 1
COURAGE

THE MOMENT

The moment
Frenetic energy,
Falling further into madness

Longing for freedom,
emerging from a shell

You have lived there for years,
locked by the hidden past

By shame and fault and guilt

From madness comes possibility

YOU ARE NOT ALONE

She spoke of pain and shadows
Haunting images and the dark stain of the
past
Of dreams that follow her, never letting go
Of anger and rage, fire and ice
The lurid stare and furtive movements,
trying to avoid the demons that linger

Pillar of strength and light, she finds beauty
in the sublime
Survivor and fighter, she walks away from
pain into the tunnel where light awaits
Proud of her ability to punch through a wall
of incomprehension
Launching into flight once more

You know the pain lingers but the other side
of that wall, it's hope and dreams

It is you. It is me.

She is not alone.

Her story lives on in the faces of scars and
creases, places others have been and can't

talk about

She opens her heart and discovers that
others feel it too.

The pain

The shame

Rising above is the next step she's taken

TERRIFYINGLY BEAUTIFUL

I knew this girl once
Her tranquil eyes and deliberate smile,
only overshadowed her thoughtful and
genuine nature
She sometimes walked away from it
The uncertainty of pain followed her
The shadows remained
She tried to speak but often the words
betrayed her
until she put pen to paper

Bringing life where darkness seemed to
dwell

Terrifyingly beautiful
And sometimes necessary
To fully embrace the pain, one must
remember
One must find a way to grow, to flourish
Writing the words is the hardest part
It's like standing on a ledge and you don't
know when you'll fall
It's like falling from that ledge but realizing
you're floating instead

Writing is one step to fill the cracks in your
armour

She protected herself, drew a line in the sand
Created barriers only she could break
But one day, she paused
She yearned for understanding
She hoped for one person to 'get her'
She opened her heart and cried for the little
girl she once was

The moments that didn't define her but
changed her and her purpose

Her journey continues even as the seasons
change
Even as the summer comes and goes
As she moves onto another path, another
journey

She will walk further and rise higher
She will remember the days of her youth and
create new memories of her adulthood

She is free to be
Free to see

Free

THE PENDULUM

The word hangs like a water droplet,
waiting to be released

Endless memories that linger

To find the meaning of this word, one must
remember

It hangs there, the clock ticking as you
anticipate its movement
A pendulum, trying to capture the moment
when it falls

Endless memories that linger

To find the meaning of this word, one must
experience the pain

If only for one moment
Pain will subside and the word will
disappear
It will fall into the darkest place, as the
water washes it away

To find the meaning of this word, one must
rewrite the story

The narrative is changing as you change

every day
You are the water droplet, longing for
release
You are the water, fluid and unwavering
You are the power within
You are beauty

You are free to dream

TWISTED MIND

Stretched and wound up
Twisted like a sponge without water
You don't have the words
to describe the beauty
But you have the words
to describe the pain

Broken and marred;
Damaged like the wing of a dragonfly
Unable to fly or describe
The lonely feeling you have
Unable to live with yourself -
And the thoughts that imprison you

Sometimes you want to end it
You yearn to end it
You feel ashamed
You have a good life, children that bring
light

Why would you end it?
How can you control the urge?

When voices in your head
keep you from thinking rationally,
you do what comes naturally

You run away from the fear
You embrace the light

YEARNS FOR LOVE

I picked up the phone and let it ring
So much to say

My throat feels constricted
Unable to breathe

What do I say?
You disappointed me
I want you to see me
To know me for the person I am

Not another statistic
Not just a girl who craves attention

I'm a girl who yearns for love
I'm a girl who loves to yearn

I'm a woman now
I long for the same things

TRAVERSING THE EDGE

A band of light traverses the night sky
Brilliant and vast
It holds a secret that cannot be defined
Captivating but lonely
You move along its noble landscape
Skirting the boundaries
Crossing it will lead to virtue
Leaving it will lead to pain
Understanding it will lead to awareness

A band of light traverses the night sky
Unknown elements of dust and stars and
blackness

Unimaginable space and time
Time has no boundary
Time is everlasting

Time is like that band of light
Traversing the edge of your life

It lasts for an eternity -
And continues into the landscape of your
mind

A BEATING HEART

A confluence of two rivers
A beating heart of competing stories
One leads to the past;
The other to the future
The present is now, the river at its deepest

You enter the water and sink effortlessly
A vision of the past
Fear in your heart

The river carries you to pain and truth

You enter the water and rise to the surface
A vision of your future
Laughter and joy in your heart

The river carries you to hope and dreams

You enter the water and wade into the
shallow side
A vision of your present
With all the undulating currents of a river
Carrying you to truth and beauty

The river is a beating heart

Following the paths of your life
Wherever it meets the beginning, it will

meet the end once more

A confluence of two rivers

Becoming one story of your life
You choose the story as you choose the river
to guide you

One story
Many truths

ONE STAR

There is one star that shines brighter than all
the rest
It is perched perfectly in the night sky
Red and bright, the colour of fire
You hold its glory like the omniscient
storyteller, enraptured
You travel millions of miles to reach that
star
In the vastness of the dark sky
You stretch your arms to the highest point
Hoping for one reply

Your request is simple
You want to touch that star and never let it
go

Never.

ONE PILL

Before you swallow it,
you imagine it moving through your body

Before the take it,
your heart beats faster, you anticipate its
effects

You imagine it taking away the crushing
feeling in your chest,
clamped tight and without resistance

When it doesn't relent,
you imagine if you should take one more

Maybe the third one or fourth will ease the
grip

When do you stop?
How long will you wait?

PART 2
REALITY

WHAT I WANT YOU TO UNDERSTAND

What I want you to understand is sometimes
the thoughts just won't go away
Days and days of relaying an event in your
head
It's like a marathon of the same thought
but instead of a finish line, it starts again

What I want you to understand is that I can't
even see the finish line
It is elusive and ephemeral, drifting further
and further from my view
Nights and nights of redirecting the thoughts
but only managing to flick a switch as you
fade away

What I want you to understand is that these
thoughts keep me awake, drive me crazy,
silently taunt me I want it to stop,
I will it to stop
but all I get in return is a recurring image

Sometimes I can close my eyes and hope to
never wake up to the torment

What I want you to understand is this person
may look fine on the outside but her insides
are screaming for silence

I want you to understand that I struggle
every day to keep these thoughts from
overtaking my mind

I am not always okay,
but I know I can fight every day.

MIRROR, MIRROR

Stifled voices and unanswered calls for help
Silent echoes of dreams unfulfilled
Stop following me, stop making me feel
special

Stop

Mirror, mirror
I ignore the reflection and stare silently at
nothing
I am nothing but an apparition, disappearing
into the abyss
I am the background of my life, memories
resurfacing and retaliating

I fight the reflection that looks unfamiliar

Who am I?

My identity is unfinished

CRUISE CONTROL

People say it's your fault
You are just like your dad -
And your kids are just like you

What a bullshit statement

Controlling one's genetics is like telling the
moon and sun to stop rising and setting.

I am who I am.

Controlling thoughts is like driving on cruise
control
You can do it with relative ease but once
you change the speed, you start to decelerate
You have to change your mind to change the
speed of the thoughts that consume you

THE JURY

A jury of your peers
Sit silently
Row upon row of silence

They mock you, pointed bony fingers
Render you unintelligible
Row upon row of silence

It doesn't make sense
In your head, people are judging you
They question your choices

Is it what you perceive?

Is it real?

Reality is elusive

It exists in the jury of your peers

The jury makes you uncomfortable

It won't leave you alone

DADS AND DAUGHTERS

Pictures of dads and daughters
Pictures of healthy dads and daughters
Climbing mountains, hiking in relative bliss

Sometimes I can't stand to look at them
Sometimes I turn away and cry
Sometimes I punch the wall

Sometimes I wish he were still alive

Always

THE CURE

Like the disease that overtakes your mind

An infection that spreads and radiates into
the roots

Your brain looks for some potion to heal,
an unction to take away the pain

Magical and sublime

It will overtake your mind,
follow you into the deepest pit where the
branches seep into the soil

It will spread further,
encompassing your entire mind and body

You feel its impact,
deep and penetrating - unaware of the
deleterious effects.

You revel in it,
you hate it,
you want it to end

You want the roots to carry you further
down -

Further into the abyss of your mind

It's not a disease,
it's a new reality of normal

You learn to adjust
Will you ever find a cure?

FEAR

Fear is like a friend that won't leave until
you demand it

Fear gives me reason to live
It creeps into my mind with anticipation

Fear looks for the most vulnerable
It draws its breath from your weakest parts

Fear is not the mind killer
It is the catalyst of the mind; it keeps you
alert and sane

Fear robs you of the ability to think logically
It breaks your sense of composure

Fear crawls along the ground, slithering its
way into your mind
It keeps you from moving forward

Fear is like an enemy that won't leave you
until you demand it

THE SECRET

The bottle holds a secret -
A secret that I will share
I want to take more than one pill -
One more to enhance the effect

It won't hurt me
It will dull the pain

It won't kill me
It will make me numb

I just want to know what it's like
For one day,
To feel normal

The bottle holds a secret

I tell it now
I hope you understand why

IMAGINE

When I see that one star shine in the sky
I imagine it's you
The silence surrounds me like the force of a
waterfall
Carrying me into that universe

With you

When I see the Milky Way
I imagine it's you
Millions of stars that shine as bright as you
did
The silence is more forceful
Like the raging waters of a river
Carrying me into its undulating currents

With you

I picture you in the space of dreams and
stars
and other things that can't be defined

Except in the silence of my heart,
sending wishes to the stars to see you once
more

REMEMBER WHEN

Remember when you were a child?

You danced in the sun
You giggled because you could
You tried to catch butterflies
You captured grasshoppers and let them go

Remember when you were a teenager?

You cried when your heart was broken
You felt alone even in the company of
friends
You wanted to scream at the injustice of the
world
You blared music that made you forget
yourself

Remember when you were in your 20's?

You wanted the world to end
You wanted the pain to stop
You did things excessively
You made mistakes and paid for them

Now you are an adult

You have experienced pain and beauty
You have loved unconditionally

You have lost people

You are damaged
Broken and brave

You face it every day
You live your truth

You are not defined by pain
But by your willingness to face it

ALIVE

The world is alive
Teaming with the sound of nature

The world is broken
Teaming with the sound of pain

The world is moving
Teaming with the sound of distractions

Your mind is alive
Teaming with the sounds of negativity

The world and your mind;
Interchangeable and circular

Teaming with frenetic energy -
And dark thoughts buried in the wake of
your dreams

OUT OF CONTROL

Like a car crash
Spinning wheels
Out of control

Thrust into a gaping hole
Widening and deepening
Swallowing your senses

Drastic, chaotic
Frenetic, frantic

Piled up and left for dead
Your mind upended

Your truth is a lie
Your pain is a band aid

Rip it off
Expose it

Pain is everywhere

DARKNESS

Darkness surrounds me;
It buries me, suffocates me

My thoughts are darker than the pain that
overwhelms me
My heart is stripped of its protective layer

It beats faster than the thoughts can leave
my brain
It keeps me trapped in a maze, detours and
pathways leading to despair

Darkness is a prisoner;
It chains me to a wall of pain

The beauty of that pain is on the other side
I can't reach it, only feel its presence

Where do I go from here?
Into the light or darkness

Only my mind knows
It betrays me all the time
until I accept it as normal

Then maybe I can let it go

Only when I feel the pain no more

LANGUIDLY

Voices echo softly
Rain gently falls
Trees sway languidly

Teardrops fall silently
Drifting away on the fleeting wind
Into a small crevice of darkness

There to remain
For eternity

LIFELINE

Open the bottle just a crack
One pill slides out -
It's a lifeline to sanity

You want to take two, maybe three
Staring, willing your hand to move forward
Stop the recurring thoughts, self-
deprecating and pervasive

People don't like you, they won't talk to you
because they know -
You're broken and other people are not

You long to slide into that pill bottle head
first -
And be swallowed up by the darkness,
finding comfort in the unknown

Where will it take you?
To a place where you feel numb;
A place where dreams become nightmares

Nightmares are real, but so is your spirit to
fight it
You punch the pills into the ground
You throw them into the receptacle of your
mind

You hate yourself -
For thinking this way,
For trying to give up

But writing these words
Is a way out of these incessant thoughts

Words have the power to transform
Words are a lifeline to sanity

The bottle is just a barrier to your dreams

WHAT ANGERS ME

I don't know what angers me more

People not calling it what it was
No, it sounded like this -
'*He was getting after you*'
Not this -
'*He was a predator; he preyed on young
girls*'
Or this -
'*He was a pedophile; he wasn't this
misunderstood man*'

He knew what he was doing

That's what angers me

IS IT MY FAULT?

The door closes -
On the other side, unabated thoughts

It is wedged shut,
firmly denying my ability to speak

Someone shouts from the other side
It's the sound of my own voice

I can't hear the words
I don't know the answer, I am denied the
answer

Is it my fault?
These thoughts hide my pain and shame

You are a child once more,
Locked away in a room with no door

A window to see your reflection
Is it really you or someone else?

How do you find the real you, the one who
wants peace in her heart?
You run and cry and escape into another
world

Acceptance was elusive then -
Except for the person who preyed upon your
childhood

Manipulated your sense of belonging – and
Made you feel special

The only value you can attribute to yourself
came from someone who did not protect you

You stare into that mirror
It betrays you, it hurts you

Cracked and broken
Damaged like the girl of the past

Fighting the demons is like drowning
The water rises and you slowly drift away

When the water recedes and you return to
the shore
*Will you recognize the girl you once were
and the adult you've become?*

Fear may dominate your mind,
but it will not dominate your heart

What the heart knew then is not what it

knows now -
It knows a child who lived in fear and an
adult who is conquering it

Light shines upon me -
It reflects the worth I give myself

Worth that cannot be taken from me;
I did not let them take it from me

The door opens to the other side
I am the voice, I hear the words

I am a survivor.

I AM AFRAID

I am afraid
Who have I become?

One moment, you imagine you're the flimsy
twig of a tree,

unable to break no matter how hard you try

The next, you are the roots, weaving in and
out of the earth, pausing for breath

Sometimes you are the bark, rough and
jagged, weathered and worn by the winds of
time

You starc at the sky from the vantage point
of your life, not certain if it's up or down

When did you lose your grip?

*Was it the moment you snapped into the
realization of your broken mind?*

Is there really something wrong with me?

You hate the person you were and maybe
even hate the person you are
You straddle on the precipice of that one
lone branch, teetering on the edge of sanity

I am afraid
I have become something different

Something beautifully unknown
Until the twig breaks and I fall
Down into the nightmares of my mind

I will be there too.

PART 3
STRENGTH

THE MOUNTAIN

The mountain wasn't the hardest to climb;
It was losing you that was hardest

Scrambling to the top
without any foothold
except a grip from your hand

Forcefully pulling me up
because you were stronger in those moments

I felt weak, trying to keep up with your
resilience
Dirt smeared our faces and I stood in awe
of you
and your brilliance

Allowing the sun to blanket your reflection
Keeping you pure of spirit

Not tainted or blemished
Like the cancer
overtaking your body

FATE

Dying is the easy part
Living without the dead is the hardest

There are many ways to die
You can choose the way you live

Hiding from everyone
You lock yourself in a room

You feel its protective shell
Surrounding and stifling you

Protection is your muse
Survival is your fate

Locking yourself
Is a choice you make

Opening the door
Your fate awaits

MOUNTAINS RISE

Mountains call
The trill sounds of a soaring bird
Languishing in the silence
Climbing sheer cliffs to rise above the
clouds

The clouds hold dreams
Perhaps hopes of times past, of the future
Where you can forget the trauma
Tuck it away where the sun never rises

Mountains echo
Dreams bounce back, reverberate
The past moves on the breeze of time
The wind leaves silence in its wake
The silence of the past you refuse to face

The mountains rise
You see the bottom, the descent unreachable
-
Falling into your past

You stand among the ruins
The mountain ripples around you
Your past falls into pieces
Nothing can rebuild it but your mind

A mind broken -
But the mountains still rise

WHISPERS

Whispers in the wind
Passes through you
Into another realm

She stands firm to the ground,
planted as the tallest tree sways in the breeze

She smiles in the genial way,
that way of capturing the right mood

She whispers to you
Where are you?
Stop focusing on the past

I can't help it
You are my past, my present, but not my
future

Wiped away as the snow melts and the
seasons change

YOU ARE NOT BROKEN

You just wanted them to hear you
One person to understand

You are not weird or strange
You are not broken

You have anxiety
You are depressed at times
You take medication

You long to talk to someone
Someone who won't judge you
Someone who *'gets'* you

ELYSIUM

You sink into the roots
It closes around you and clamps your chest
Breath leaves you as quickly as the rain
seeps into the ground
You reach for that rain, that one drop of
water
You yearn for one drop to take you to
another place
Elysium, where you can live without
yourself

The one that brings you pain

THE FUTURE

Rushing, roaring
The river strips you of the past
The future is eroded as the stones fade into
obscurity
Blackness is what you remember
A closed door to your memories
The river gets deeper and darker,
As you follow the currents to your future

Unknown destination
The river will not give up its secrets -
And neither will you

SURVIVAL

A million stars go out at once
A million dreams extinguished
A million broken thoughts

A thousand whispers in your ear
A thousand misinterpretations
A thousand tears to drown the pain

A hundred envious ways to believe
A hundred self-deprecating words
A hundred scars from the wounds

Stars and dreams and tears, infused as one
simple word

Survival

THE CHRYSALIS

Like the chrysalis,
she is moving through different stages
Opening paths to beauty and pain

She lives for these moments when she can
explore the perfect words
Words to describe the power of emerging
from a cocoon

Words to encapsulate her pain, words that
describe her universal shift
She is recreating herself every day, as the
moon waxes and wanes

She can live the life she was meant to live,
one in which the pain of the past is
overtaken by the beauty of the sunset
The sun will rise, a new day will emerge -
she is reborn into a new plane of existence

She walks through the pain and the
memories

And every moment is one she faces with the
courage of a butterfly,
embracing where the wind will take her

TRANSLUCENT

Your mind is wrapped in translucent
material
Stretched and worn, opaque and pale
You enter the darkness of forests and
caverns
No one enters but you and your empty shell

You fill your time with memories of the past
Stories you construct from the pain of grief
and loss and shame
You recreate and relive and resign yourself
to the truth

You are broken in the most beautiful way
You can tell a thousand stories to a thousand
people
But it all starts at the same place

A place of raw emotion
Of uncertainty and unpredictability
Masking the pain of childhood
Opening the frantic nature of your mind

You were once a child of unimaginable
potential
Poised to take on the world
You were smart and brave and independent

What happened? When did you fall?
It was a moment, a blemish
You were scarred then as you are now

There will always be hills to climb

One day, you slide into the worst parts of
you
They become the best parts
The ones you long to forget but can't
Because it will always be there
In your soul
But it will not consume you

You make the choice to live and fight
Because that choice is your own

THE HAWTHORN TREE

Standing tall, but alone
A penetrating smell in the silence
Once stripped of its regal nature,
It now enjoys reckless days

When did it first fall
Into obscurity, into winter's bliss
It was alone then, without companionship
Now it breathes in the transient air

A moment of sun wakes it
A blossoming flower only hopes to spread
wider,
To embrace the elements of the weather and
wait for warmth
A lone petal, opens to the air and finds peace
amongst the nesting birds.

It stands tall and alone
Proud and uninhibited
Obscure and breathless

It is alone.
It lives.

STORY OF ME

It's my narrative, my story
No one can change that
Except me

I write when the pain comes
But I also look for beauty
Where do I find it?

In the dreams of children
In the winds the blow fiercely
In the tree that stands firm

FAIRYTALES

It's a fairytale I imagine
There is an ogre and he wants to save a
beautiful princess

This is my Dream,
the image that I create

The ogre is my mind
The princess is my heart

But I don't need saving from an ogre
I can save myself

The ogre is not welcome anymore
The door is closed

The princess demands it
She reclaims her identity, her power

She can look in the mirror
See her reflection
Not recoil from the pain

UNFINISHED

Unfinished business
Is what they call it

Trauma is unfinished business
It is a cycle of repetitive thoughts
You attempt to shred them
Shredding them changes the narrative
You can't put it back in order
It is now mixed and jumbled

Changing a pattern is hard
A pattern becomes a puzzle -
The puzzle creates an image -
The image is your own

You can change the narrative
You make it your story

You are in control now

IMAGES

You change the narrative,
But how will you write about it

You have lived with the pain;
You have used it to construct the image of
your life

You wrench the pain from your heart
You draw upon the traumatic experience of
your childhood
The pain that allows you to feel and live
those emotions

What does it take to recreate?
An image forms in your mind, one that
twists and turns
Into strength and resilience, into a positive
realm
This is where your heart belongs

After the narrative of your former life,
This is where you need to be